MW01075081

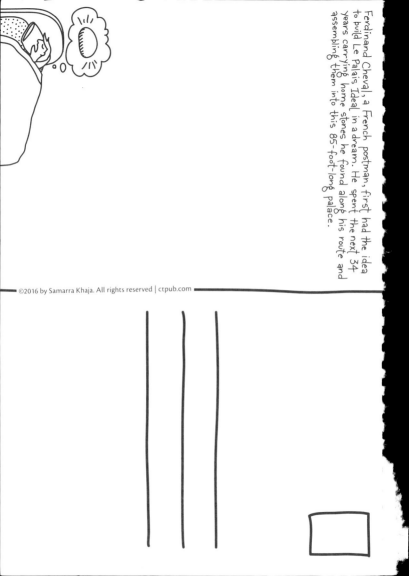

Ferdinand Cheval, a French postman, first had the idea to build Le Palais Idéal in a dream. He spent the next 34 years carrying home stones he found along his route and assembling them into this 85-foot-long palace.

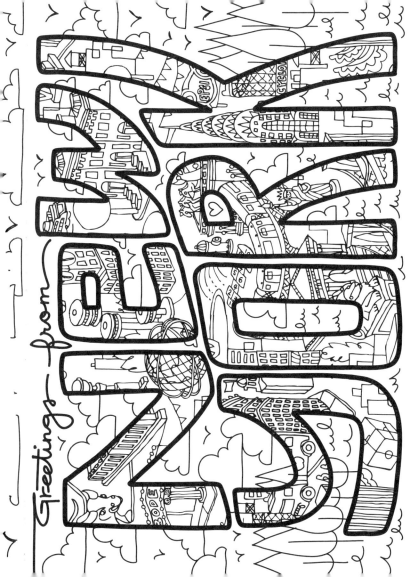

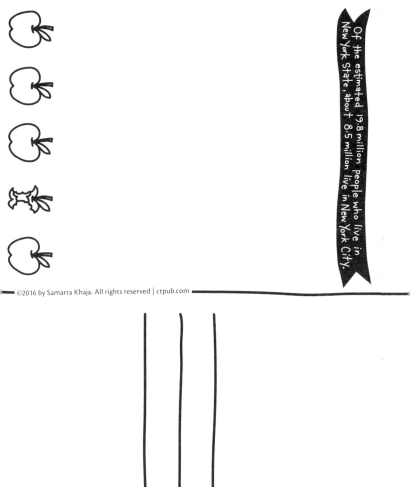

Of the estimated 19.8 million people who live in New York State, about 8.5 million live in New York City.

I ♥ NY

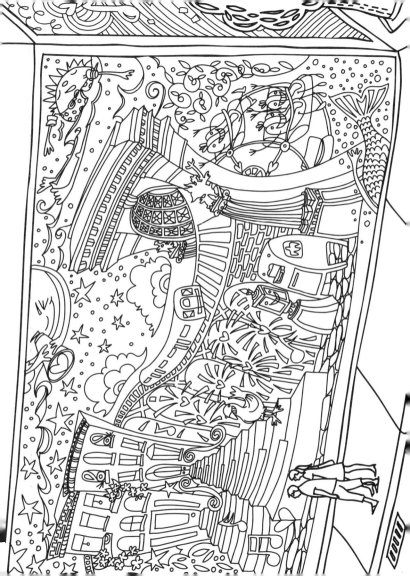

Life-size mural drawn by the artist (that's me!) called "Heartbeat Brooklyn." It can be found at the corner of 12th Street and 2nd Avenue in New York City and can be spotted from the southbound F train, if you keep your eyes peeled!

At over 65 feet high, 60 feet long, and 18 feet wide, Lucy is the world's largest "elephant"—actually a small building in Margate City, New Jersey, she has contained business offices, a restaurant, a tavern, and now a museum over her 135-year life.

Las Vegas is a city known for its neon lights, and some of the most famous—including Caesars Palace, Binion's Horseshoe, and the Golden Nugget—have ended their days at the Neon Boneyard, with over 200 other signs to keep them company.

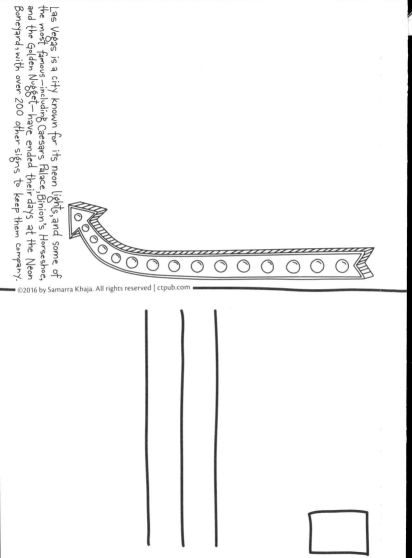

How do you take down half a house? Very carefully! 54½ Saint Patrick Street is the only building remaining from what was once a row of six town houses in Toronto. The exterior wall was once a dividing wall between 54½ and its neighbor.

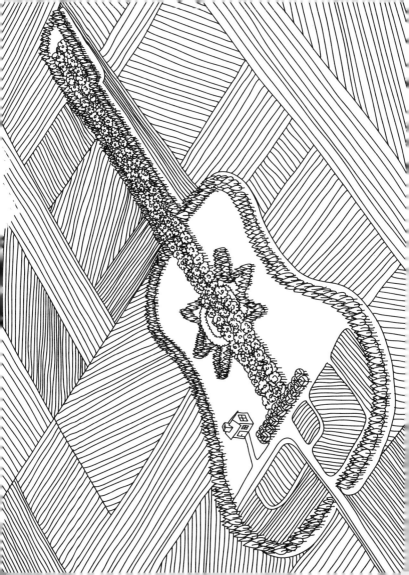

A farmer in Laboulaye, Argentina, planted a guitar-shaped forest to honor his late wife's love of the instrument. It stretches two-thirds of a mile and can be seen from outer space.

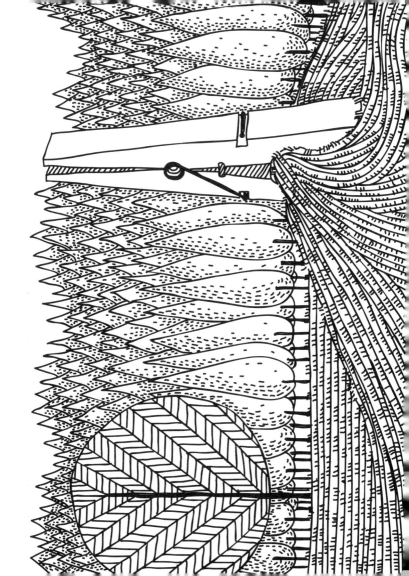

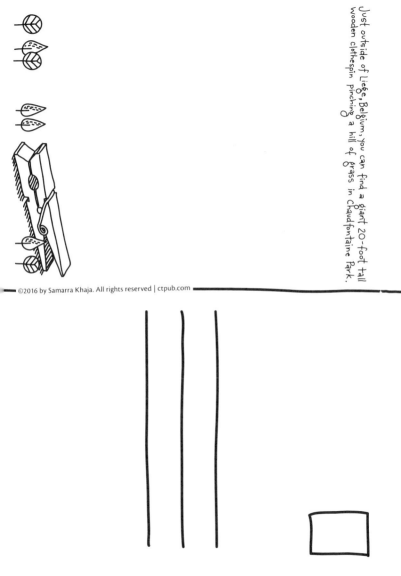

Just outside of Liège, Belgium, you can find a giant 20-foot tall wooden clothespin pinching a hill of grass in Chaudfontaine Park.

Fitzroy Gardens' Fairies Tree, carved from 1931 to 1934 by writer Ola Cohn, is dedicated to the children of Melbourne and is adorned with magical fairies, elves, pixies, and Australian animals.

Built in the late 1940s, the Model Tudor Village at Fitzroy Gardens includes scale models of William Shakespeare's home and Anne Hathaway's cottage among the little buildings.

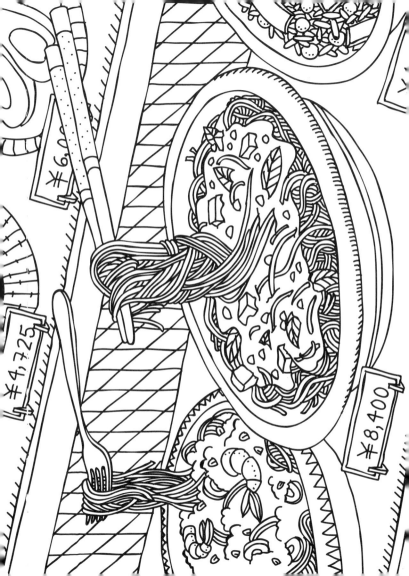

¥6,000

¥4,725

¥8,400

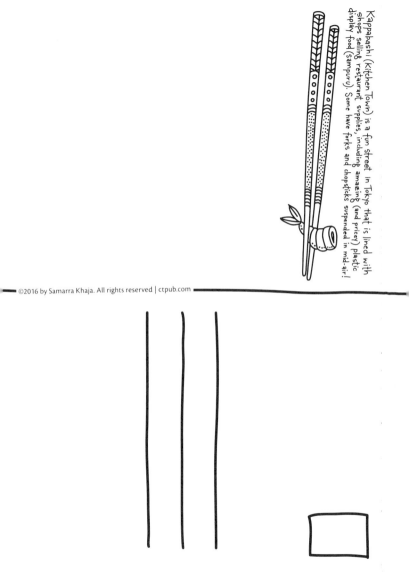

Kappabashi (Kitchen Town) is a fun street in Tokyo that is lined with shops selling restaurant supplies, including amazing (and pricey) plastic display food (sampuru). Some have forks and chopsticks suspended in mid-air!

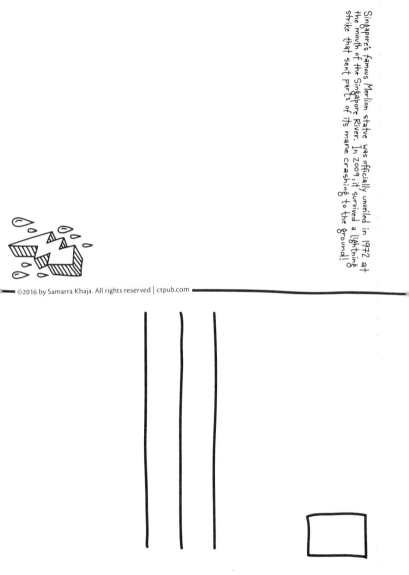

Singapore's famous Merlion statue was officially unveiled in 1972 at the mouth of the Singapore River. In 2009, it survived a lightning strike that sent parts of its mane crashing to the ground!

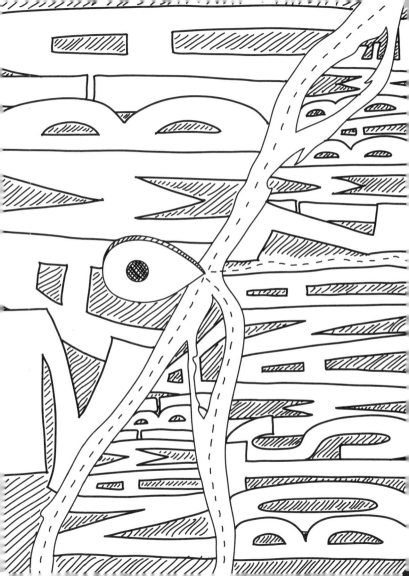

1! 2! 3! 4!

The African Quadripoint, as it's called, is the only place in the world where the borders of four countries meet!

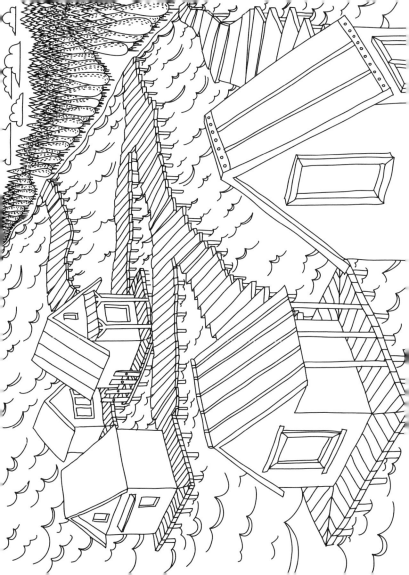

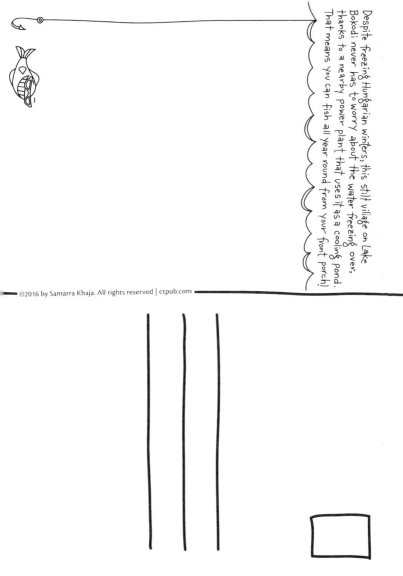

Despite freezing Hungarian winters, this stilt village on Lake Bokodi never has to worry about the water freezing over, thanks to a nearby power plant that uses it as a cooling pond. That means you can fish all year round from your front porch!

Commissioned in 1632, Agra's Taj Mahal was constructed by the hands of more than 22,000 people, including masons, painters, stonecutters, inlayers, carvers, calligraphers, and embroidery artists. Today, the biggest group of non-tourists you'll find basking on the mausoleum grounds are families of rhesus macaques, one of India's best-known Old World monkey species.

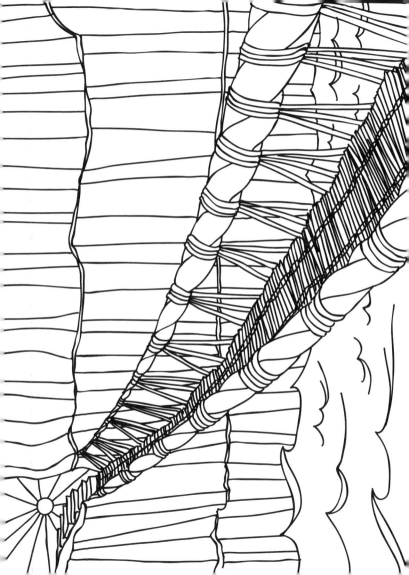

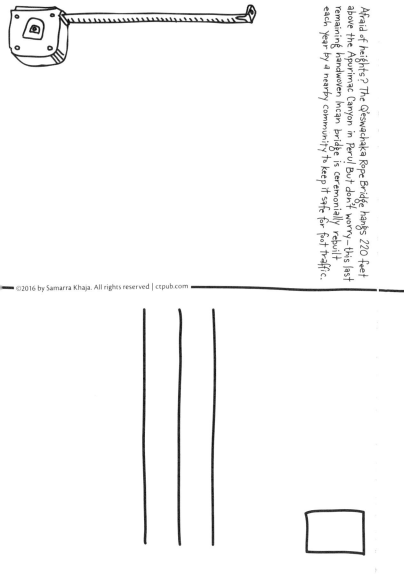

Afraid of heights? The Q'eswachaka Rope Bridge hangs 220 feet above the Apurimac Canyon in Peru! But don't worry—this last remaining handwoven Incan bridge is ceremonially rebuilt each year by a nearby community to keep it safe for foot traffic.

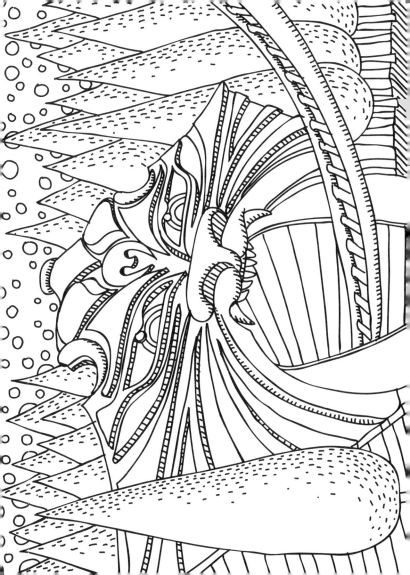

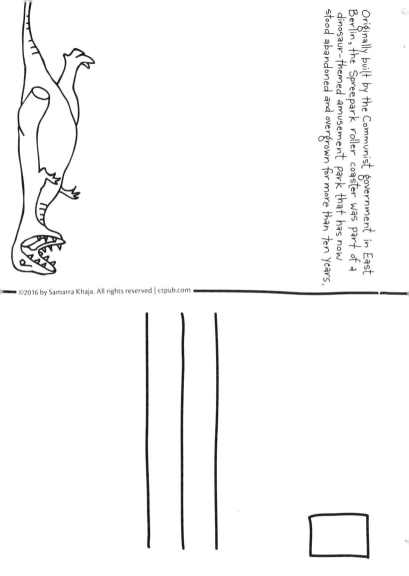

Originally built by the Communist government in East Berlin, the Spreepark roller coaster was part of a dinosaur-themed amusement park that has now stood abandoned and overgrown for more than ten years.

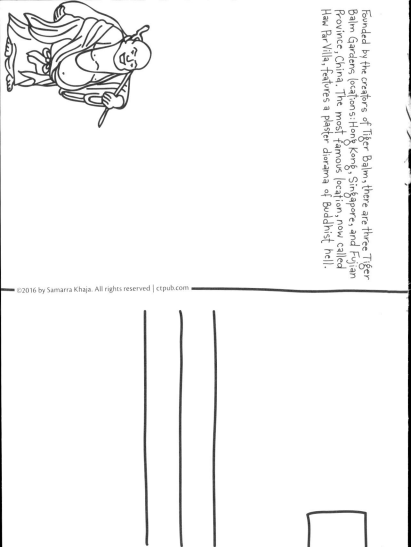

Founded by the creators of Tiger Balm, there are three Tiger Balm Gardens locations: Hong Kong, Singapore, and Fujian Province, China. The most famous location, now called Haw Par Villa, features a plaster diorama of Buddhist hell.

Bahrain's Tree of Life, the only tree in miles of desert with no visible source of water, is over 400 years old and stands on a sandy mound formed over a 500-year-old fortress.

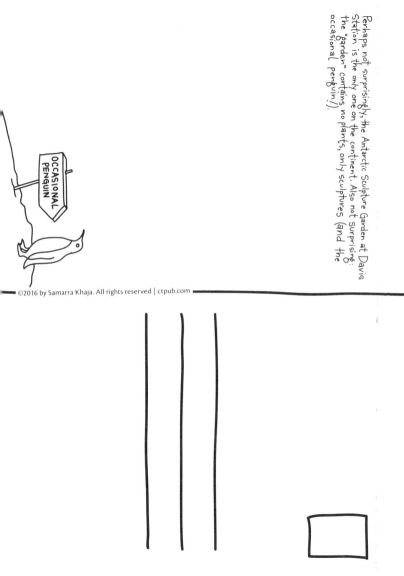

OCCASIONAL PENGUIN

Perhaps not surprisingly, the Antarctic Sculpture Garden at Davis Station is the only one on the continent. Also not surprising: the "garden" contains no plants, only sculptures (and the occasional penguin!).

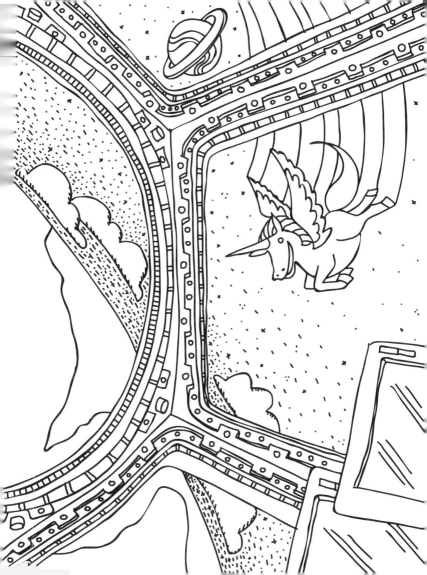

Sure, it's pricey (an estimated $150 billion to build), but there's no denying that the International Space Station is THE best seat in the house to gaze at our beautiful planet. Plus, you might even spot a unicorn, because who knows what's out there!

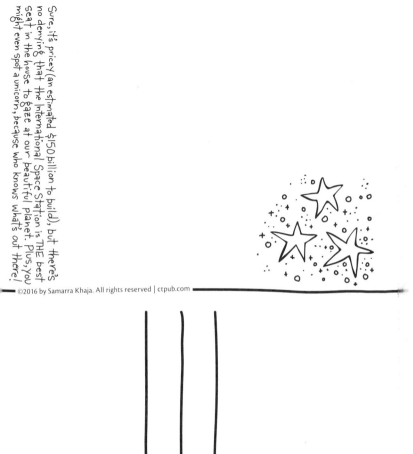

Hi
Mom!